W9-AHU-524

# planet
# EARTH

# Earth's
# Ecosystems

## By Jim Pipe

**Science curriculum consultant: Suzy Gazlay, M.A.,
science curriculum resource teacher**

**Gareth Stevens**
Publishing

Please visit our web site at www.garethstevens.com.
For a free catalog describing our list of high-quality books, call 1-800-542-2595 (USA) or 1-800-387-3178 (Canada). Our fax: 1-877-542-2596

Library of Congress Cataloging-in-Publication Data available upon request from the publisher.

ISBN-13: 978-0-8368-8916-1 (lib. lbg.)
ISBN-10: 0-8368-8916-9 (lib. bdg.)
ISBN-13: 978-0-8368-8923-9 (softcover)
ISBN-10: 0-8368-8923-1 (softcover)

This North American edition first published in 2008 by
**Gareth Stevens Publishing**
A Weekly Reader® Company
1 Reader's Digest Road
Pleasantville, NY 10570-7000 USA

This U.S. edition copyright © 2008 by Gareth Stevens, Inc. Original edition copyright © 2007 by ticktock Media Ltd. First published in Great Britain in 2007 by ticktock Media Ltd., Unit 2, Orchard Business Centre, North Farm Road, Tunbridge Wells, Kent, TN2 3XF United Kingdom

ticktock Project Editor: Ruth Owen
ticktock Picture Researcher: Ruth Owen
Project Designer: Emma Randall
With thanks to: Mark Sachner, Suzy Gazlay and Elizabeth Wiggans, Elaine Wilkinson and Matt Harding

Gareth Stevens Editor: Jayne Keedle
Gareth Stevens Creative Director: Lisa Donovan
Gareth Stevens Graphic Designer: Alex Davis

Photo credits (t = top; b = bottom; c = center; l = left; r = right):
Photography by Bruce Elliot and JL Allwork
Ingo Arndt/Minden Pictures/FLPA: 29tr. Jim Brandenburg/Minden Pictures/FLPA: 19bl. Nigel Cattlin/FLPA: 17br. Digital Stock: 9cbr. R. Dirscher/FLPA: 22/23 main Gerry Ellis/Minden Pictures/FLPA: 6bl. Chris Fallows/ apexpredators.com: 14t. Michael & Patricia Fogden/Minden Pictures/ FLPA: 20tl. Michio Hoshino/Minden Pictures/ FLPA: 10br. David Hosking/FLPA: 21b, 27cr. iStock: 4/5. Thomas Lazar/naturepl.com: 27tr. NASA/ESA: 22tl. OSF/Photolibrary Group: cover. Fritz Polking: 25br. Michel Roggo/naturepl.com: 11bl. Science Photo Library: 17bc. Shutterstock: title page all, 3, 4l, 4 inset x3, 5 inset x4, 6tl x4, 6–7 main, 7tl, 7cr x2, 9tl, 9tr, 9 ctr, 9br, 9bl, 10t, 12 all, 13t, 14b all, 15 main, 15tr, 15cr, 16–17 main, 16tl, 16b x 3, 17cr, 17bl, 18, 19cl, 19tr, 19cr, 26t, 26c, 26b, 27tr, 27c, 27b, 28l x3, 28/29 main, 29br, 30 all, 31 all. Jurgen & Christine Sohns/FLPA: 8, 19br. Superstock: 15br, 20 main, 22b, 23cr, 24bl, 25tr, 25cr, 26cl. Hayley Terry: 13b. Ticktock Media Archive: 11tl, 21t.

Printed in the United States of America

1 2 3 4 5 6 7 8 9 10 09 08 07

# CONTENTS

*A woodland is a large ecosystem with many plants and animals.*

*Your body is a small ecosystem. Inside you there are thousands of tiny organisms. These include the bacteria that help you digest your food.*

# CHAPTER 1:
# What Is an Ecosystem?

An ecosystem is a place in which a community of living things rely on each other for survival. Your home is a sort of ecosystem. Your family and pets depend on each other, and the home, for food, water, and shelter.

## ECOSYSTEMS

An ecosystem supports a community, or group, of living things. Different plants and animals in an ecosystem depend on each other for survival. They also depend on nonliving things, such as sunshine, soil, and water. Ecosystems can be as enormous as the Sahara Desert or as small as a pond.

*A single oak tree can be an ecosystem.*

*An oak tree can support a community of birds, beetles, and fungi (above).*

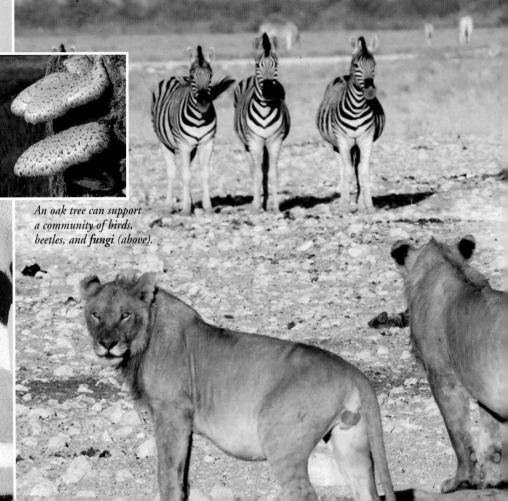

## WHAT IS A HABITAT?

The word **habitat** refers only to the place in an ecosystem in which a plant or an animal lives. For example, a fish and a mud worm may be part of the same river ecosystem. However, the fish's habitat is the water in the river, while the worm's habitat is the mudflat alongside the river.

## WHAT IS A BIOME?

Scientists divide Earth into large areas called **biomes.** Each biome has a particular **climate** and similar plants and animals. Each type of biome on our planet is found in many parts of the world. Everything that lives in a biome is suited to the climate and soil in that region. A biome includes many ecosystems, or smaller communities of plants and animals.

## EXAMPLES OF BIOMES

**POLAR REGIONS**
Polar regions make up one kind of biome. The climate is very cold, windy, and dry. Almost no plants can survive. Animals such as polar bears, seals, and penguins get their food from the sea.

**MOUNTAIN REGIONS**
Mountain regions make up another biome. Mountains are cold, windy, and wet. Over a certain height, it is so cold that trees will not grow. That height is called the tree line.

**DESERTS**
The desert biome is very hot and dry. Desert plants and animals are able to survive with very little water.

*Savannas are a type of biome found in South America and Africa. The African savanna is home to many kinds of wildlife and has many ecosystems. Here, a pride of lions is hunting zebras. Both animals are part of the same ecosystem.*

## DON'T GO NEAR THE WATER!

All living things need water to survive. Changes in water supplies affect how animals live. Piranhas live in rain forest rivers in South America. During the wet season, they are usually **scavengers.** In the dry season, piranhas turn into hunters. As the water levels go down, big groups of piranhas are forced to cluster in small patches of water. Together, they will attack large animals that come to the river to drink.

## WHAT MAKES A PERFECT HOME?

Animals living in an ecosystem are affected by their **environment**. In a desert, animals and plants must work hard to find and store water. It's no surprise, then, that fewer plants and animals live in desert biomes. In the rain forest, however, water is plentiful and life abundant.

## BIOTIC OR ABIOTIC

An ecosystem is made up of both living and nonliving factors. Animals and plants are living things and are called **biotic factors.** Soil, water, sunlight, and weather are all nonliving. Those are known as **abiotic factors.**

Abiotic factors have a huge effect on an ecosystem. Almost all ecosystems depend on the Sun. Green plants use sunlight to convert water and carbon dioxide into food. That process, called **photosynthesis,** also produces oxygen. Without the Sun, plants would have no food and we would have no oxygen!

**ABIOTIC FACTORS**

**LIGHT AND HEAT**
The Sun provides the energy plants need to make food. The Sun's energy also keeps animals warm.

**SUNLIGHT**
In a shady wooded area, some grasses and other plants don't get enough sunlight for photosynthesis.

**WATER**
Without water there would be no life.

*Look at this picture of Monument Valley in Arizona. What abiotic factors can you see here? Compare the abiotic factors in this ecosystem with the abiotic factors where you live.*

## PLANTS AND ABIOTIC FACTORS

**Materials needed**
- bean seeds
- potting soil
- 4 plastic plant pots
- watering can

1) Fill each plant pot with potting soil. Plant a bean seed in each pot, just below the surface of the soil. Label the pots A, B, C, and D.

2) Place pots A and B in a bright, sunny spot. Put pots C and D in a dark corner.

3) Water only pots A and C every day.

> **i** Which plant do you think will grow best? It should be plant **A**, which gets both light and water. Plant **C** doesn't get enough light, and plant **B** doesn't get water. Without light or water, plant **D** may not grow at all!

### SOIL
Soil provides important **nutrients** that help plants grow. It also holds water for plants and animals to use.

### ATMOSPHERE
Our **atmosphere** is the giant blanket of air around Earth.

### SHELTER
Cracks in a rock or an old wall provide shelter for snails, ants, wasps, and other tiny creatures.

*Light and heat from the Sun help the grass grow.*

*Zebras feed on the grass and provide food for lions.*

*In a well-balanced ocean ecosystem, sea otters and kelp (seaweed) help each other survive.*

## THE ECOSYSTEM JIGSAW

An ecosystem is like a seesaw. All the living and nonliving parts must be in balance. If there's not enough rain on the African savanna, the grass withers and dies. Without enough grass to eat, zebras die too. In turn, that's bad news for lions, because zebras are the lions' **prey**.

If sea otters left an area of the ocean, the **sea urchins** they eat would increase in number. The sea urchins would then eat so much seaweed that the **kelp forest** would die. With no kelp forest in which to hide from sharks and other **predators**, sea otters would not return to the area. A habitat would have been destroyed, and an ecosystem changed forever.

## PESKY RABBITS

Humans often bring new plants or animals to an ecosystem. That can upset the balance. In 1859, Thomas Austin released 24 rabbits on his farm in Australia. With no foxes to hunt them, the number of rabbits exploded. There are now almost 300 million rabbits in Australia! They eat so many plants that a lot of native animals find it hard to survive.

## A TEAM EFFORT

A healthy ecosystem has many different species living in it. Each species helps keep the ecosystem working. If one group of animals or plants disappears, the whole system can break down. Introducing a new species into an ecosystem can be equally damaging. Nature, however, has many ways of keeping a balance. If one animal or plant **population** becomes too big, it is often reduced by a lack of food, by predators, by **drought**, or by disease.

*Nature has its own way of keeping ecosystems balanced. Forests choked by overgrowth are cleared by forest fires. That makes way for healthy new growth.*

**Keep an ecosystem journal for one week.**

1) List all the ecosystems you see around you. Keep in mind that an ecosystem can be as large as your backyard or as small as the patch of soil beneath a rock!

2) Write down all the biotic factors you see, such as specific types of plants and animals. Also note abiotic factors. Those may include soil, a pond, or another water source. Even a trash can is a possible food source for wild animals.

3) Can you think of some ways that you fit into these ecosystems? Do you feed the birds? Water plants in your garden? Does your home also provide a home for birds or insects?

How do the different members of the ecosystems around you depend on one another? How do they help each other?

# CHAPTER 2:
# Living in an Ecosystem

**Plants and animals change over time to survive in their environment. That process is known as adaptation.**

Different plants and animals depend on different abiotic factors. Many plants thrive in sunlight. Others do better in a cool, shady area beneath a tree. Plants have a better chance of surviving if they need different abiotic factors. It means they are not competing for the same, possibly limited, resources.

## POPULATIONS

The population of each animal species may vary in size. Each time a particular population gets bigger or smaller, its effect on the rest of the ecosystem changes. All of the different populations in an ecosystem make up the community.

*Moss often grows on trees. It grows best when the abiotic factors in its environment include dampness and shade.*

# NICHES

A **niche** describes the role that a plant or animal plays in its environment. An animal's niche tells something about how it behaves and what it needs to survive. Different animals and plants fit into the ecosystem in different ways. Having a niche often means they aren't competing for the same resources.

*Pandas feed almost entirely on bamboo. Eating a plant that almost no other animal in its ecosystem feeds on helps pandas survive. It gives pandas a special niche in their ecosystem.*

## WINTER BREAK

Many animals have adapted over millions of years. These adaptations help them find food, hide from predators, or survive in a particular habitat. In winter, for instance, bears are less active and sleep more. This is called **hibernation.** During hibernation, a bear uses less energy. That enables it to eat less in winter, when food is scarce.

## GETTING ALONG

Many animals and plants share an ecosystem. They make space for themselves in different ways.

### SPREADING OUT

In a tropical rain forest, animals avoid competing with each other by living at different levels. Birds live in treetops. Monkeys live in branches. Leopards and other large animals spend most of their time on the forest floor.

### KEEPING A LOOKOUT

Many animals live in groups or herds. That helps keep them safe. While some animals eat, others can keep an eye out for danger. Lions and wolves hunt in groups. That helps them bring down large prey.

### MARKING TERRITORY

Many animals are territorial. They don't like to share their space with other animals, not even those of their own species. A tiger scratches a tree to mark its territory. That warns off other tigers.

# WEB OF LIFE

The living things in an ecosystem are linked together by **food chains**. Food chains tell you who eats whom. Plants are most often on the bottom of the food chain. Plants are known as **producers**. They use the Sun's energy to make their own food. That nutrition is passed on to **consumers**. Plant-eating animals are known as primary consumers. They, in turn, are eaten by secondary consumers, which eat meat. At the top of the chain are big predators, such as lions and sharks. They are third-level, or tertiary, consumers.

Food chains are part of a larger **food web**. A food web shows how different food chains interact with one another. Members of the same food web may compete with one another for food.

*Sharks and other tertiary consumers get lots of energy from eating meat. They need it. Catching a seal is hard work!*

## FOOD WEBS

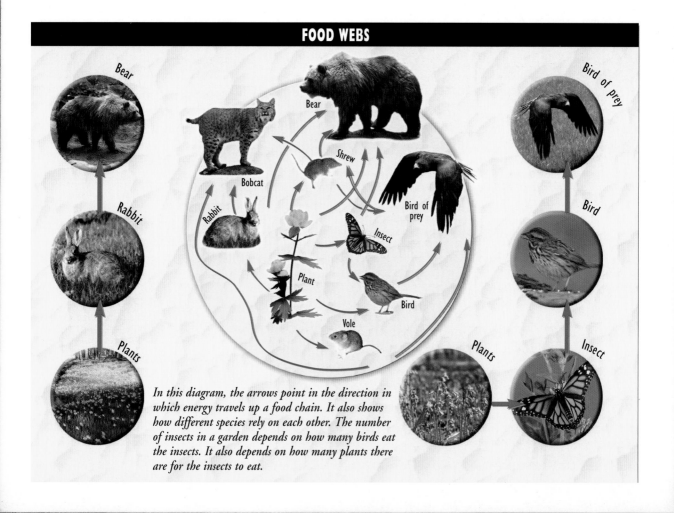

*In this diagram, the arrows point in the direction in which energy travels up a food chain. It also shows how different species rely on each other. The number of insects in a garden depends on how many birds eat the insects. It also depends on how many plants there are for the insects to eat.*

## IT'S A DIRTY JOB, BUT SOMEBODY'S GOT TO DO IT!

An elephant munches away all day, but much of what it eats goes straight through it! So why is the ground in an elephant's habitat not knee-deep in **dung**? Animals and plants known as **decomposers** feed on droppings. They break down the waste of other living things. Decomposers also break down dead organisms. Bacteria and fungi do most of the hard work. They are helped by maggots (usually fly **larvae**), dung beetles, and earthworms. Decomposers speed up the process of decay, or rot. In this way, they help put nutrients back into the soil.

*Two dung beetles roll a ball of manure. They will either eat it or lay their eggs inside it.*

## PREDATORS AND THEIR PREY

Every ecosystem has predators with different ways to catch their prey.

### CHEETAHS

Cheetahs can run more than 60 miles (100 kilometers) per hour. However, the chase tires them. They often have to rest for 20 minutes before they eat their kill.

### A PREDATOR PLANT

Unlike most plants, the Venus flytrap is not at the bottom of the food chain. It eats insects. The plant has short, stiff trigger hairs on its leaves. When an insect touches a trigger hair, the leaf snaps shut, trapping the insect. The plant has digestive juices to dissolve the insect's soft parts.

## SCAVENGER'S DELIGHT

Scavengers are animals that eat dead animals and break them into little pieces. Those include flies, wasps, ravens, cockroaches, and even raccoons. Scavengers help start the process of decomposition. Vultures are well-known scavengers. Here, a vulture has begun tearing apart the body of a dead cow.

# CHAPTER 3:
# Natural Cycles

**Ecosystems are not just about animals eating each other. Plants and animals also need sunlight, water, carbon, nitrogen, and energy to live. These elements are recycled again and again.**

## THE ENERGY CHAIN

Animals can't produce their own food. Some animals get their energy by eating plants. Other animals get their energy by chomping on animals that have eaten plants. But the energy chain doesn't stop there. Plants and animals release waste throughout their lives. It may be in the form of gases and the waste products of digestion. Waste materials return energy to the environment. When plants and animals die, they decay and add nutrition to the soil.

*Plants use sunlight to turn air and water into sugars. The sugars are used as food by plants and by the animals that eat the plants. This giraffe gets its energy from leaves high in the treetops.*

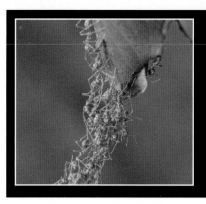

## BIG BIOMASS!

The combined weight of a species or type of organism is called its **biomass**. Humans may dominate the animal world, but we make up less than 0.5 percent of all animal biomass. All the ants in the world probably weigh at least 20 times more than all the humans!

## TOP OF THE HEAP

An **ecological pyramid** shows how energy moves up the food chain. As energy flows through an ecosystem, some of it gets lost along the way. For example, animals lose energy when they lose heat from their bodies. Since there is less energy farther up the food chain, there are also fewer animals near the top of the chain.

## AN ORCA'S ECOLOGICAL PYRAMID

Orca

Seals

Fish

Krill (small shrimp-like animals)

Phytoplankton (tiny drifting animals and plants)

*Orcas (killer whales) are at the top of their food chain. They are much bigger than fish and other organisms below them. In terms of biomass, however, the combined weight of all the organisms the orcas eat is greater than the weight of all the orcas.*

## ENERGY: FROM THE SUN TO YOUR TABLE

1. Corn plants use energy from the Sun to turn air and water into sugars. The sugars are used by the plant as food. Energy in the sugars is passed on to animals that eat the plant.

2. A field of corn uses energy from the Sun to grow. The corn is picked when it is ripe.

3. Corn grown for animals to eat is loaded into silos or other feeding bins. Ears of corn produced as food for people end up at grocery stores.

4. Steaming-hot corn on the cob provides energy, flavor, and fun!

*Elephants need huge quantities of water to carry nutrition to every part of their large bodies. They spend a great deal of their time near water supplies.*

## WATER

Water is essential for life. You could survive for many weeks without food, but you would last only a few days without water. Water helps carry nutrients throughout the bodies of organisms and helps carry out waste. About 70 percent of an adult human's body is made up of water!

The water on our planet is constantly going through a process called the **water cycle**. Water moves from the oceans up into the atmosphere as **water vapor**. It returns to the land, and the cycle begins again.

There will never be any more water on Earth than there is now. All the water on our planet is used over and over again. The raindrops falling on your head may contain the same water that fell on the dinosaurs more than 65 million years ago!

## THE CARBON CYCLE

Carbon is an **element** found in every living thing. It is also found in many nonliving things. Plants absorb carbon dioxide from the atmosphere during photosynthesis. They then use the carbon to make **carbohydrates**. When animals eat plants, the carbon is passed on. Humans and animals give off carbon dioxide gas when they breathe out. They put carbon back into the atmosphere.

*Animals are living stores of carbon. When they die, most of the carbon returns to the atmosphere. All dead plants and animals contribute important nutrients and other substances to the soil when they die.*

## THE WATER CYCLE

**THIS DIAGRAM SHOWS ALL THE STAGES OF THE WATER CYCLE.**

*2. The warm water vapor (gas) rises in the air, where it cools and forms tiny droplets. This is called* **condensation.** *The droplets mass together to form clouds.*

*3. As the drops get heavier, they fall as rain or snow. This is called* **precipitation.**

*4. Rivers carry the rainwater back to the sea. The process of water gathering on Earth is called* **accumulation.**

*1. The Sun warms the sea's surface, causing the water to turn into vapor. This is called* **evaporation.**

## WHAT'S FOR DINNER, MOM?

Salmon die so that their young can live. Soon after adult salmon **spawn** (lay their eggs), they die. Their rotting bodies add nutrients to the water. That's not enough to satisfy the appetites of growing salmon, however. These kids eat the bodies of their dead parents!

## MAKE YOUR OWN WATER CYCLE

**Materials needed**

- large plastic bowl
- jug of water
- plastic wrap
- a small plastic container
- string or large rubber band

1) Place a small container in the center of a large plastic bowl.

2) Pour some water into the small container.

3) Stretch a sheet of plastic wrap over the bowl. Fasten it snugly with a piece of string or a large rubber band.

4) Place the bowl in a sunny place.

The Sun will heat the water and cause it to evaporate, or turn into water vapor. The vapor will rise into the "atmosphere" above the water in the bowl. If the plastic sheet is cool, the vapor will condense into water droplets. These droplets will fall, like "rain," into the bowl. You have created a miniature water cycle!

## THE NITROGEN CYCLE

There's more to manure than meets the nose. Decomposing dung is part of the nitrogen cycle. Nitrogen is a gas. It makes up 78 percent of Earth's atmosphere. All living things use nitrogen to help build protein.

Plants and animals can't process this gas, but they do soak up **nitrates** from the ground. Nitrates contain nitrogen. Bacteria, **lichens**, and algae turn nitrogen in the air and soil into nitrates. Nitrates help plants grow. When cows eat grass, they consume nitrates. Their waste then returns nitrates to the soil, and the cycle continues.

*Dung makes our whole world greener. Without it, we would need more artificial fertilizer for our crops. We'd also have less nitrogen in the atmosphere.*

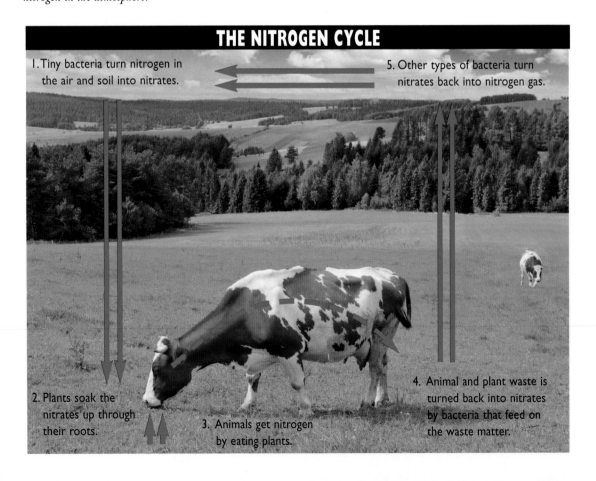

**THE NITROGEN CYCLE**

1. Tiny bacteria turn nitrogen in the air and soil into nitrates.

2. Plants soak the nitrates up through their roots.

3. Animals get nitrogen by eating plants.

4. Animal and plant waste is turned back into nitrates by bacteria that feed on the waste matter.

5. Other types of bacteria turn nitrates back into nitrogen gas.

*Artificial nitrates in the soil can get into our drinking water and the atmosphere. Some scientists think that nitrates are linked to diseases such as cancer and asthma.*

## TOO MUCH OF A GOOD THING

Farmers use nitrates as fertilizers to grow more crops. People have developed ways of making artificial nitrates. Artificial nitrates, however, can overload the natural system. As a result, they may hurt the ecological balance. Too many nitrates in rivers and lakes can increase algae growth. The algae then use up oxygen in the water, killing fish and other wildlife.

## THE MINERAL CYCLE

Animals and plants also need **minerals**, such as phosphorus, iron, sulfur, and calcium. Many of these minerals form in rocks deep underground. The minerals are brought to the surface by volcanoes. On land, most animals get minerals from the water they drink. In the sea, shellfish take calcium from the water. The shellfish use the calcium to make their shells.

## THE MINERAL CYCLE

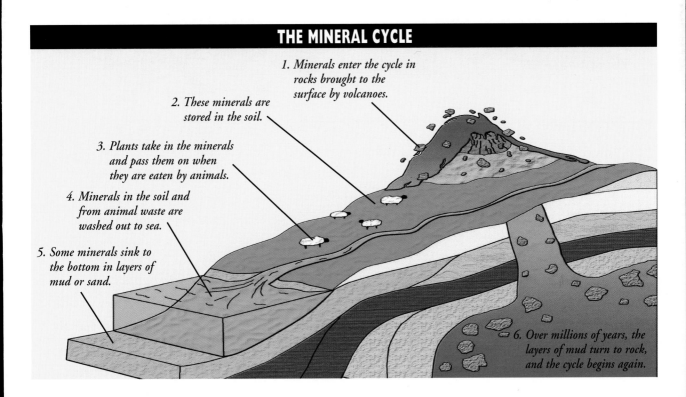

1. Minerals enter the cycle in rocks brought to the surface by volcanoes.

2. These minerals are stored in the soil.

3. Plants take in the minerals and pass them on when they are eaten by animals.

4. Minerals in the soil and from animal waste are washed out to sea.

5. Some minerals sink to the bottom in layers of mud or sand.

6. Over millions of years, the layers of mud turn to rock, and the cycle begins again.

# CHAPTER 4:
# Biomes

**The world is divided into large regions called biomes. Every place on Earth is part of a biome. Most biomes support a wide variety of plant and animal life. Others, such as the polar regions of Antarctica and the Arctic, are so extreme that a limited number of species have adapted to life there.**

*The Arctic provides polar bears with plenty of seals and fish for their diet. People who live in the bears' habitat also provide a source of food—garbage!*

*Central American rain forests are a perfect home for the glasswing butterfly. It feeds on the nectar of tropical plants.*

## LIFE ON LAND

Let's take a walking tour of some of Earth's biomes. We'll start at the equator.

You're probably in a rain forest biome. Tropical rain forests are hot and very rainy for much of the year. As you walk north, it is still hot but rains less. That's where you find the subtropical forests of India and the dry savanna of East Africa. You'll also hit the Everglades, the subtropical wetlands of Florida. Farther north, you come across hot, dry deserts in Africa, Asia, and North America. **Temperate** grasslands and deciduous forests await you in Europe, North America, and Asia. Those biomes have warm summers and cold winters.

As you approach the North Pole, you see cone-bearing evergreens, such as pines. These are part of the great northern conifer forests that stretch across Asia and North America. Finally, you reach the cold deserts of the tundra and the icy Arctic regions.

# EARTH'S BIOMES

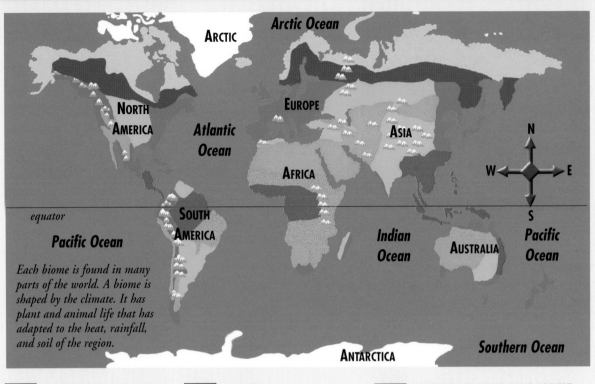

Each biome is found in many parts of the world. A biome is shaped by the climate. It has plant and animal life that has adapted to the heat, rainfall, and soil of the region.

**TEMPERATE GRASSLANDS**
*Warm, dry summers, cool or cold winters; rainfall supports lots of plant and animal life*

**SAVANNA**
*Large plains with scattered trees and bushes; amount of plant life determined by amount of rainfall*

**DESERT**
*Dry land, little rain; plant life includes cacti, which store water*

**TUNDRA**
*Cold, windy plains; soil freezes just below surface; plants need short roots to absorb nutrients*

**ARCTIC/ANTARCTICA**
*Extremely cold and dry all year; frozen ground and icy seas; little plant life*

**OCEAN**
*Saltwater environment supports a huge variety of marine life*

**TEMPERATE DECIDUOUS FOREST**
*Shrubby coastal area; plants and animals adapted to hot, dry summers and mild winters*

**CONIFEROUS FOREST**
*Cold evergreen forest; most animals migrate or hibernate in winter*

**TROPICAL RAIN FOREST**
*Hot, wet climate that supports a huge variety of life*

## ISLAND WONDERS

Islands often have unique ecosystems. For example, lemurs live only on Madagascar, off the coast of Africa. The marine iguana (pictured here) and giant tortoises live only on the Galápagos Islands in the Pacific Ocean. The marine iguana is the only seagoing lizard in the world. It dives in the sea to find seaweed to eat.

## LIFE IN THE WATER

The oceans make up the largest biome on our planet. Ocean food webs here contain everything from giant whales to microscopic organisms called **phytoplankton**.

The ocean needs the Sun to give its animal and plant communities food and energy. Billions of phytoplankton float near the surface of the ocean. They use light from the Sun to make food for themselves. Then they become food for bigger animals. Through the ocean food webs, the Sun's energy is passed on.

### THE BLUE PLANET

Earth is often called the Blue Planet. This photograph from space shows why. About 70 percent of Earth's surface is covered by water.

### AN INLAND SEA

Lake Baikal is a freshwater sea in Russia. It is frozen for more than five months a year. Yet underneath the ice, there is a remarkable ecosystem. A species of freshwater seal, called the nerpa, is the lake's only mammal. The nerpa can hold their breath for more than an hour! Many species of fish live just below the lake's icy surface.

Compared with saltwater, freshwater is rare on our planet. Just 0.3 percent of Earth's freshwater flows as rivers or sits in lakes. Most of the planet's freshwater is frozen as ice at the North and South poles and in **glaciers**. Ponds, rivers, and lakes are all rich freshwater ecosystems. Their communities often get energy and food from producers on land.

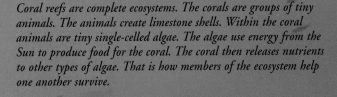

*Coral reefs are complete ecosystems. The corals are groups of tiny animals. The animals create limestone shells. Within the coral animals are tiny single-celled algae. The algae use energy from the Sun to produce food for the coral. The coral then releases nutrients to other types of algae. That is how members of the ecosystem help one another survive.*

## WATER ECOSYSTEMS

### THE OCEANS

The ocean biome contains many ecosystems. Ecosystems have developed even in the deepest parts of Earth's oceans. There, animals are adapted to life in the dark. The anglerfish swims around with a lighted, fleshy "fishing rod" on its head. When the light attracts other fish, the anglerfish quickly snaps them up.

### RIVERS

Five thousand species of fish live in the Amazon River, in South America. One inhabitant of this river ecosystem is the electric eel. It stuns its prey with an electric shock. The Amazon River community includes many other predators, such as freshwater dolphins, otters, turtles, and giant snakes.

## EXTREME BIOMES

There are ecosystems everywhere on Earth, even in the most extreme biomes. In Antarctica, for example, cold temperatures freeze exposed human flesh in seconds. Yet the animals that live there have adapted to their environment. Teleost fish, for instance, live in icy polar waters. Their bodies make a chemical that keeps their blood from freezing.

At the other extreme is the baking heat of a desert. In desert biomes, plants such as cacti can survive years of drought on water collected from a single rainfall. Animals such as kangaroo rats, snakes, and lizards are busy at night to avoid the daytime heat. During the day, they lie in burrows or under rocks.

Mountains are home to a wide range of plants and animals that can survive sudden changes in temperature. As you climb up a mountain, the climate, soil, and plant life change over very short distances.

### LIFE AT INCREDIBLE DEPTHS

At least 1 mile (1.6 km) beneath the ocean surface, hot water gushes from deep-sea vents. This water is loaded with minerals. Bacteria use the heat and minerals to make food. The bacteria and the food they produce are part of a food web that includes the tubeworm (below). The tubeworm lives on the food created by the bacteria. Tubeworms form protective tubes around themselves. The tubes can grow to lengths of 10 feet (3 meters) or more.

*The cardon cactus is the largest cactus in the world. It grows in the Sonoran Desert, in the southwestern United States and Mexico. The cardon's trunk can store more than a ton of water at one time. Its branches point up. That means less of the plant's surface is exposed to direct sunlight.*

## SURVIVING EXTREME CONDITIONS

### SPADEFOOT TOAD

The spadefoot toad lives in deserts in North America. It avoids the heat by hibernating underground most of the year.

### BACTRIAN CAMEL

The Gobi Desert in central Asia combines freezing winters with short, hot summers. The Bactrian camel can survive both seasons. In winter, it grows a thick coat and gets water from snow. In summer, the camel can go for months without water.

### EMPEROR PENGUINS

Emperor penguins mate and lay eggs in the winter, when Antarctic temperatures are as low as −40° Fahrenheit (−40°Celsius). For more than two months, the male bird stands in freezing conditions keeping the egg warm. The male emperor penguins huddle close together for warmth.

# CHAPTER 5:
# Changing Ecosystems

When left to themselves, farmers' fields and backyards alike soon become covered with weeds. Taller plants arrive and choke the grass, and different species take over as the ecosystem develops. The order in which new life comes into a habitat and joins an ecosystem is called succession.

## RECLAIMING A HABITAT

A lot of forest land that is now filled with plants and animals was buried under glaciers for centuries. The glaciers have now retreated slowly back to the Arctic. After a glacier has retreated, it usually takes hundreds of years for the land to be fully reclaimed by nature.

## THE BIRTH OF AN ISLAND

Above water, the rough surface of a coral reef is not an ideal place for plants and animals to live. Over time, however, the reef's limestone shell is worn away by wind and rain. The rock breaks into small grains that become soil. Seeds blow onto the reef and settle in the soil. They

*The Saskatchewan Glacier (above) is in Banff National Park in Canada. The glacier has not fully receded yet. In places where the glacier has receded, plants are taking hold (below).*

*Aldabra is a coral island in the Indian Ocean. This remote island is home to a very large number of animal and plant species, including endangered species. The few people who live there are scientists.*

### FOREST FIRES: A NEW BEGINNING?

Many plants and animals have adapted to fire. Fires do not mean the end of forest ecosystems. The heat of a forest fire causes pinecones to burst open, scattering thousands of seeds to the ground. New grasses sprout (right). Woodpeckers and other birds return to feed on beetles and other insects that have moved into burned trees.

grow into plants. When the plants die, their waste makes the soil even richer. That enables larger plants to grow, which in turn provide food and shelter for animals. In time, what was once an uninviting habitat can become a tropical island where many species live.

*Just about any surface will give way to a habitat's original plant life if left alone for long enough!*

## NEW SPECIES IN YOUR BACKYARD

**Materials needed**
• container (an empty aquarium tank or a soda bottle)
• sample of pond water

1) Collect a sample of pond or rainwater and put it in a large clear container. Leave it in direct sunlight.
2) Look at the water every day. You will probably see that algae are quick to move in!

3) Check the water every few days with a magnifying glass. You may also spot other small organisms in the water. For an even better look, examine samples of water in a shallow dish.
4) If you'd like new life to come more quickly, add small pieces of dried grass and other plant material to the container.

This experiment shows how new species might appear in a new habitat. Often the first to arrive are algae, microscopic organisms that drift around in the air until they find a pond or damp place to live in.

## WHAT CAN WE DO?

### MAKING ROOM FOR WILDLIFE

Cities are ecosystems, too. Areas of wasteland can be turned into wildlife meadows. Garden ponds and trees provide food and shelter for many small animals.

PLEASE TAKE NOTHING BUT PICTURES LEAVE NOTHING BUT FOOTPRINTS

### WATER = LIFE

As Earth's human population grows, our planet is running out of freshwater. Many people are battling to save wetlands, rivers, and lakes. They want to attract animals and other wildlife back to their original habitats.

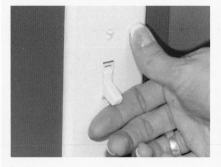

### SAVING ENERGY HELPS

You can get involved! Turn off lights when you are not using them, or lower the heat at home. Every time you do these things, you use less energy. Saving energy reduces the demand for oil, gas, or coal. Earth has only a limited supply of such resources.

## HUMANS AND ECOSYSTEMS

In the last 200 years, humans have had a huge impact on ecosystems all over the planet. Today, Earth's ecosystems are more threatened than at any other time in human history. The tropical rain forest, for example, is being cut down to clear space for farming. That activity destroys animal and plant habitats. Some rain forest plants may have uses as medicines or food. If those plants are destroyed, we will never know how they might have helped humans.

The burning of fossil fuels, such as coal and oil, has polluted the atmosphere. Modern farms have replaced woodlands. Weed killers and bug sprays poison both the soil and wildlife. Decomposers cannot easily break down plastics and other products made by humans.

Individual species have little or no time to adapt to the sudden changes resulting from human activity. That's why species are being wiped out faster than at any other time in the past 10,000 years. We need to find new ways to live that leave ecosystems in balance.

Healthy ecosystems are good for all living things. They provide us with the food we eat. They also provide us with clean air and water. Perhaps even more important, they assure the survival of the planet for generations to come.

*The growth of towns, cities, and farmland can divide wildlife communities. Today, only two populations of mountain gorillas survive in Africa. These two groups live in two separate areas of a national park. The two areas are 28 miles (45 km) apart.*

*Are garbage dumps the next ecosystem? With dumps the size of this landfill, it may be just a matter of time before a variety of organisms move in. Few of them are likely to be ones that we would welcome!*

## TOO HIGH A PRICE FOR SUCCESS?

The Alaska pipeline helps transport oil across vast distances. However, many people say it spoils the beauty of the landscape and harms wildlife. The pipeline has disturbed the migration routes of herds of caribou, also called reindeer. In turn, this affects wolves and other predators that depend on the migrating caribou for food.

# GLOSSARY

**abiotic factors:** nonliving parts of an ecosystem, such as water, sunlight, soil, climate, or rocks

**accumulation:** process of water gathering on Earth

**adaptation:** process by which a plant or an animal changes over time to suit its surroundings

**atmosphere:** thick layers of air that surround Earth and contain gases such as nitrogen and oxygen

**biomass:** combined weight of a species or type of organism

**biome:** large region with similar climate, weather, and plant and animal life. Examples of biomes are rain forest, ocean, and desert.

**biotic factors:** living parts of an ecosystem, such as plants and animals

**carbohydrates:** sugars and starches found in many foods. They are made up of carbon, hydrogen, and oxygen.

**climate:** the average weather in an area over a long period of time

**condensation:** process by which a gas, such as water vapor, changes into a liquid

**consumer:** an organism that eats other organisms

**decomposer:** an organism, such as a fungus, that breaks down dead organisms, returning nutrients to the environment

**dung:** animal droppings

**drought:** unusually long period without rainfall

**ecological pyramid:** a way of showing how energy is lost as it goes up the food chain. Millions of animals or plants are at the bottom of the chain. Far fewer can live at the top.

**ecosystem:** a natural system made up of a community of plants and animals

**element:** a substance made up of a single type of atom

**environment:** objects and conditions, such as climate, soil, and living things, that surround and act on a habitat

**evaporation:** the process by which a liquid (such as water) turns into a gas (such as water vapor)

**food chain:** the relationship between plants and animals that shows who eats what and whom

**food web:** a set of linked food chains in an ecosystem

**fungi:** a group of organisms such as mushrooms, molds, and yeast

**glacier** a large body of ice that moves slowly down a slope or valley or spreads out on the surface of the land

**habitat:** a specific area, small or large, that is home to a plant or animal

**hibernation:** a state of rest, or dormancy

**kelp forest**: underwater forest of tall, brown seaweed. Kelp is a type of algae.

**krill:** shrimp-like creatures found in huge numbers in open seas

**larvae:** the young of insects and amphibians. Larvae hatch from eggs and often look different from adults.

**lichen:** a plant that is a combination of a fungus and an alga

**mineral:** a solid, usually inorganic (nonliving) substance that occurs naturally on Earth

**niche:** a unique role in an ecosystem. The niche of a bee, for example, is to pollinate flowers, which helps the plant to reproduce.

**nitrate:** a chemical compound that contains nitrogen

**nutrients:** minerals and substances that plants and animals need to grow and develop

**organism:** a living thing

**photosynthesis:** the process by which plants use the energy in sunlight to convert carbon dioxide and water into food (carbohydrates)

**phytoplankton:** microscopic floating plants

**pollute:** to dirty or poison a place or the atmosphere

**population:** all the animals in one species that live in an ecosystem

**precipitation:** the process by which water falls to the ground as rain, hail, sleet, or snow

**predator:** an animal that lives by killing and eating other animals

**prey:** an animal that is hunted or eaten for food by another animal

**producer:** an organism that uses the Sun's energy to make its own food

**scavengers:** animals that feed on the bodies of animals that are already dead

**sea urchins:** sea animals with bodies covered with spines. Many sea urchins are ball-shaped.

**spawn:** to produce or fertilize eggs

**succession:** the order in which plants and animals colonize a habitat

**temperate:** having a climate that is mild. It is not too hot or too cold.

**water cycle:** the constant movement of water from the air to land and back to the air

**water vapor:** a gas that is produced when water evaporates